For Love
of the
Rockies

Photography by
Celia Roberts

For Celia Roberts moving to Colorado in 1969 was the rediscovery of a love affair, not only of the Rocky Mountains, but also of photography. Although picture-taking had been a part of her life since her childhood in Kentucky, it was spending quality time in the mountains that woke her to the possibility of doing professionally what she had loved doing so much "just for fun."

What this realization led to was the opening of Reflections Gallery in Vail in 1974 where Celia's work was sold for the next eight years. During that time she held one-woman shows in Vail, Denver, and at her alma mater, Hanover College in Indiana. Celia won several awards in regional competitions.

At present, Celia is living in Boulder, Colorado, where she continues her work in artistic nature photography, known for its distinctive painting-like quality. She has also expanded into the area of photo journalism, primarily by traveling in the developing world where she has had the opportunity to photograph the "more human side of our existence."

"For me photography has been about learning how to see ... and by seeing, I mean becoming increasingly aware of the subtle beauty in nature and in our lives. For instance, the way light and shadow play across a meadow, the look on a father's face as he watches his daughter at her wedding, or the subtle gestures of love made by those who otherwise have very little in their lives.

"When we begin to see such beauty in simple things, then our lives become far more magical, more satisfying. We tend to focus on the 'not so beautiful' in our world and I feel we are not getting the total picture. Through my photographs I want people to be gently reminded of those simple beautiful things which surround each of us, and to be more deeply in touch with our relationship and commitment to one another, worldwide."

Celia's photographs are presently available at the Handworks, Boulder; Susan Anderton Gallery, Crested Butte; Steamboat Art Company, Steamboat Springs; The Earthworks, Denver; Uniquely Colorado, Winter Park; The Marmot's Tail, Vail; Trimble Court Artisans, Ft. Collins; and Redstone Art Center, Redstone in Colorado.

© **Earth Images** ISBN 0-9620621-1-1

June morning on Piney Lake, Colorado.

Stamp

©1989 For Love of the Rockies Series I, **Earth Images,** Box 1217, Boulder, CO 80306, (303) 499-7434

Winter along the Flatirons, Boulder, Colorado.

Stamp

©1989 For Love of the Rockies Series I, **Earth Images,** Box 1217, Boulder, CO 80306, (303) 499-7434

Autumn aspen in Eagle County, Colorado.

Stamp

© 1989 For Love of the Rockies Series I, **Earth Images,** Box 1217, Boulder, CO 80306, (303) 499-7434

Columbine cluster near Crested Butte, Colorado.

Stamp

©1989 For Love of the Rockies Series I, **Earth Images**, Box 1217, Boulder, CO 80306, (303) 499-7434

Winter shadows near Vail, Colorado.

Stamp

©1989 For Love of the Rockies Series I, **Earth Images,** Box 1217, Boulder, CO 80306, (303) 499-7434

Fall on Independence Pass near Aspen, Colorado.

Stamp

© 1989 For Love of the Rockies Series I, **Earth Images,** Box 1217, Boulder, CO 80306, (303) 499-7434

Aspen leaves, Rabbit Ears Pass near
Steamboat Springs, Colorado.

Stamp

© 1989 For Love of the Rockies Series I, **Earth Images**, Box 1217, Boulder, CO 80306, (303) 499-7434

A winter moon near Durango, Colorado.

Stamp

©1989 For Love of the Rockies Series I, **Earth Images**, Box 1217, Boulder, CO 80306, (303) 499-7434

Cabin on Cement Creek, Gunnison County, Colorado.

Stamp

© 1989 For Love of the Rockies Series I, **Earth Images,** Box 1217, Boulder, CO 80306, (303) 499-7434

The Great Sand Dunes, Southern Colorado.

Stamp

© 1989 For Love of the Rockies Series I, **Earth Images,** Box 1217, Boulder, CO 80306, (303) 499-7434

Winter on Vail Pass, Colorado.

Stamp

© 1989 For Love of the Rockies Series I, **Earth Images,** Box 1217, Boulder, CO 80306, (303) 499-7434

Changing aspen on Kebler Pass, Colorado.

Stamp

© 1989 For Love of the Rockies Series I, **Earth Images**, Box 1217, Boulder, CO 80306, (303) 499-7434

Maroon Bells, Aspen, Colorado.

Stamp

© 1989 For Love of the Rockies Series I, **Earth Images,** Box 1217, Boulder, CO 80306, (303) 499-7434

Garden of the Gods, Colorado Springs, Colorado.

Stamp

© 1989 For Love of the Rockies Series I, **Earth Images**, Box 1217, Boulder, CO 80306, (303) 499-7434

Fall grasses in Chaffee County, Colorado.

Stamp

© 1989 For Love of the Rockies Series I, **Earth Images,** Box 1217, Boulder, CO 80306, (303) 499-7434

Afternoon light in the aspen, Vail, Colorado.

Stamp

©1989 For Love of the Rockies Series I, **Earth Images**, Box 1217, Boulder, CO 80306, (303) 499-7434

Young buck near Castle Peak, Colorado.

Stamp

© 1989 For Love of the Rockies Series I, **Earth Images**, Box 1217, Boulder, CO 80306, (303) 499-7434

Chair 2 and the Gore Range, Vail, Colorado.

Stamp

©1989 For Love of the Rockies Series I, **Earth Images**, Box 1217, Boulder, CO 80306, (303) 499-7434